Davy Crockett

Published in the United States of America by Cherry Lake Publishing
Ann Arbor, Michigan
www.cherrylakepublishing.com

Content Adviser: Ryan Emery Hughes, Doctoral Student, School of Education, University of Michigan
Reading Adviser: Marla Conn MS, Ed., Literacy specialist, Read-Ability, Inc.
Book Design: Jennifer Wahi
Illustrator: Jeff Bane

Photo Credits: © Melinda Fawver/Shutterstock, 5; © North Wind Picture Archives / Alamy Stock Photo, 7; © anthony Heflin/Shutterstock, 9, 22; © Don Smetzer / Alamy Stock Photo, 11; © Kent Weakley/Shutterstock, 13; © Niday Picture Library / Alamy Stock Photo, 15, 23; © Fotosearch / Stringer/Getty, 17; © Everett Historical/Shutterstock, 19; © C. Stuart/Library of Congress, 21; Cover, 6, 12, 18, Jeff Bane; Various frames throughout, Shutterstock Images

Library of Congress Cataloging-in-Publication Data

Names: Haldy, Emma E., author. | Bane, Jeff, 1957- illustrator.
Title: Davy Crockett / Emma E. Haldy ; illustrated by Jeff Bane.
Description: Ann Arbor : Cherry Lake Publishing, 2017. | Series: My
   itty-bitty bio | Includes bibliographical references and index. |
   Audience: Grades K-3.
Identifiers: LCCN 2016031794| ISBN 9781634721516 (hardcover) | ISBN
   9781634722834 (pbk.) | ISBN 9781634722179 (pdf) | ISBN 9781634723497
   (ebook)
Subjects: LCSH: Crockett, Davy, 1786-1836--Juvenile literature. |
   Pioneers--Tennessee--Biography--Juvenile literature. | Legislators--United
   States--Biography--Juvenile literature. | United States. Congress.
   House--Biography--Juvenile literature. | Alamo (San Antonio, Tex.)--Siege,
   1836--Juvenile literature.
Classification: LCC F436.C95 H35 2017 | DDC 976.804092 [B] --dc23
LC record available at https://lccn.loc.gov/2016031794

Printed in the United States of America
Corporate Graphics

About the author: Emma E. Haldy is a former librarian and a proud Michigander. She lives with her husband, Joe, and an ever-growing collection of books.

About the illustrator: Jeff Bane and his two business partners own a studio along the American River in Folsom, California, home of the 1849 Gold Rush. When Jeff's not sketching or illustrating for clients, he's either swimming or kayaking in the river to relax.

I was born in 1786. I lived in Tennessee.

I had eight brothers and sisters.

5

I enjoyed the outdoors. I liked to hunt. I did not like school.

7

I ran away from home when I was 13 years old.

I worked. I explored the American **frontier**.

What part of the world would you like to explore? Why?

I came home to help my father.

I got married. I had six children.

I joined the Tennessee **militia**.
I served for two years.

I proved that I was a strong
leader.

13

I decided to become a **politician**. I enjoyed serving my community.

I loved telling stories. I was famous for my speeches.

Do you like to tell stories?
Why or why not?

I tried to do what I thought was right. Not everyone agreed with me.

I lost some **elections**. I was tired of politics. I decided to try something new.

I wanted to move to Texas.
It was part of Mexico.

Texans wanted freedom.
They had started a war.

I joined the fight. I died in the Battle of the Alamo.

I was an adventurous man. I had an exciting life. I loved the frontier!

What would you like to ask me?

1799

1780

Born
1786

1821

1880

Died
1836

23

glossary

elections (i-LEK-shuhnz) system of choosing leaders by voting

frontier (fruhn-TEER) the far edge of a country

militia (muh-LISH-uh) a group of people who are trained to fight but are not soldiers

politician (pah-li-TISH-uhn) a person elected to the government

index